ON THE SEXUAL THEORIES OF CHILDREN

BY

SIGMUND FREUD

British Library Cataloguing-in-Publication Data
A catalogue record for this book is available from the
British Library

Contents

Sigmund Freud

Sigismund Schlomo Freud was born on 6th May 1856, in the Moravian town of Příbor, now part of the Czech Republic.

Sigmund was the eldest of eight children to Jewish Galician parents, Jacob and Amalia Freud. After Freud's father lost his business as a result of the Panic of 1857, the family were forced to move to Leipzig and then Vienna to avoid poverty. It was in Vienna that the nine-year-old Sigmund enrolled at the Leopoldstädter Kommunal-Realgymnasium before beginning his medical training at the University of Vienna in 1873, at the age of just 17. He studied a variety of subjects, including philosophy, physiology, and zoology, graduating with an MD in 1881.

The following year, Freud began his medical career in Theodor Meynert's psychiatric clinic at the Vienna General Hospital. He worked there until 1886 when he set up in private practice and began specialising in "nervous disorders". In the same year he married Merth Bernays, with whom he had 6 children between 1887 and 1895.

In the period between 1896 and 1901, Freud isolated himself from his colleagues and began work on developing the basics of his psychoanalytic theory. He published *The Interpretation of Dreams*, in 1899, to a lacklustre reception, but continued to produce works such as *The Psychopathology of Everyday Life* (1901) and *Three Essays on the Theory of Sexuality* (1905). He held a weekly meeting at his home known as the "Wednesday Psychological Society" which eventually developed into the Vienna Psycho-Analytic Society. His ideas gained momentum and by the end of the decade his methods were being used internationally by neurologists and psychiatrists.

Freud made a huge and lasting contribution to the field of psychology with many of his methods still being used in modern psychoanalysis. He inspired much discussion on the wealth of theories he produced and the reactions to his works began a century of great psychological investigation.

In 1930 Freud fled Vienna due to rise of Nazism and resided in England until his death from mouth cancer on 23rd September 1939.

ON THE SEXUAL THEORIES
OF CHILDREN
(1908)

The material on which the following synthesis is based
is derived from several sources. Firstly, from the direct
observation of what children say and do; secondly, from
what adult neurotics consciously remember from their
childhood and relate during psycho-analytic treatment; and
thirdly, from the inferences and constructions, and from the
unconscious memories translated into conscious material,
which result from the psycho-analysis of neurotics.

That the first of these three sources has not by itself
supplied all that is worth knowing on the subject is due
to the attitude which the adult adopts towards the sexual
life of children. He does not credit them with having any
sexual activity and therefore takes no trouble to observe
any such thing while, on the other hand, he suppresses
any manifestation of such an activity which might claim
his attention. Consequently the opportunity of obtaining
information from this, the most unequivocal and fertile
source of all, is a very restricted one. Whatever comes from the
uninfluenced communications made by adults concerning
their own conscious childhood memories is at the best subject
to the objection that it may have been falsified in retrospect;

but, in addition to thus, it has to be viewed in the light of the fact that the informants have subsequently become neurotic. The material that comes from the third source is open to all the criticisms which it is the custom to marshal against the trustworthiness of psycho-analysis and the reliability of the conclusions that are drawn from it. Thus I cannot attempt to justify it here; I can only give an assurance that those who know and practise the psycho-analytic technique acquire an extensive confidence in its findings.

I cannot guarantee the completeness of my results, but I can answer for the care taken in arriving at them.

There remains a difficult question to decide. How far may one assume that what is here reported of children generally is true of all children - that is, of every particular child? Pressure of education and varying intensity of the sexual instinct certainly make great individual variations in the sexual behaviour of children possible, and, above all, influence the date at which a child's sexual interest appears. For this reason, I have not divided my presentation of the material according to the successive epochs of childhood, but have combined into a single account things that come into play in different children sometimes earlier and sometimes later. It is my conviction that no child - none, at least, who is mentally normal and still less one who is intellectually gifted - can avoid being occupied with the problems of sex in the years *before* puberty.

4

I do not think much of the objection that neurotics are a special class of people, marked by an innate disposition that is 'degenerate', from whose childhood life we must not be allowed to infer anything about the childhood of other people. Neurotics are people much like others. They cannot be sharply differentiated from normal people, and in their childhood they are not always easily distinguishable from those who remain healthy in later life. It is one of the most valuable results of our psycho-analytic investigations to have discovered that the neuroses of such people have no special mental content that is peculiar to them, but that, as Jung has expressed it, they fall ill of the same complexes against which we healthy people struggle as well. The only difference is that healthy people know how to overcome those complexes without any gross damage demonstrable in practical life, whereas in nervous cases the suppression of the complexes succeeds only at the price of costly substitutive formations - that is to say, from a practical point of view it is a failure. In childhood neurotic and normal people naturally approximate to each other much more closely than they do in later life, so that I cannot regard it as a methodological error to make use of the communications of neurotics about their childhood for drawing conclusions by analogy about normal childhood life. But since those who later become neurotics very often have in their inborn constitution an especially strong sexual instinct and a tendency to precocity and to a premature expression of that instinct, they make it possible for us to recognize a great deal of infantile activity more sharply and clearly than our capacity for observation (which is in any case a blunted one) would enable us to do in other children. But we shall of course only be able to assess the true value of these communications made by neurotic adults when, following Havelock Ellis's example, we shall have thought it worth while to collect the childhood memories of *healthy* adults as well.

In consequence of unfavourable circumstances, both of an external and an internal nature, the following observations apply chiefly to the sexual development of one sex only - that is, of males. The value of a compilation such as I am attempting here need not, however, be a purely descriptive one. A knowledge of infantile sexual theories in the shapes they assume in the thoughts of children can be of interest in various ways - even, surprisingly enough, for the elucidation of myths and fairy tales. They are indispensable, moreover, for an understanding of the neuroses themselves; for in them these childish theories are still operative and acquire a determining influence upon the form taken by the symptoms.

If we could divest ourselves of our corporeal existence, and could view the things of this earth with a fresh eye as purely thinking beings, from another planet for instance, nothing perhaps would strike our attention more forcibly than the fact of the existence of two sexes among human beings, who, though so much alike in other respects, yet mark the difference between them with such obvious external signs. But it does not seem that children choose this fundamental fact in the same way as the starting-point of their researches into sexual problems. Since they have known a father and mother as far back as they can remember in life, they accept their existence as a reality which needs no further enquiry, and a boy has the same attitude towards a little sister from whom he is separated by only a slight difference of age of one or two years. A child's desire for knowledge on this point does not in fact awaken spontaneously, prompted perhaps by some inborn need for established causes; it is aroused under the goad of the self-seeking instincts that dominate him, when - perhaps after the end of his second year - he is confronted with the arrival of a new baby. And a child whose own nursery has received no such addition is able, from observations made in other homes, to put himself in the same situation. The loss of his parents' care, which he actually experiences or justly fears, and the presentiment that from now on he must for evermore share all his possessions with the newcomer, have the effect of awakening his emotions and sharpening his capacities for thought. The elder child expresses unconcealed hostility towards his rival, which finds vent in unfriendly criticisms of it, in wishes that 'the stork should take it away again' and occasionally even in small attacks upon the creature lying helpless in the cradle. A wider difference in age usually softens the expression of this primary hostility. In the same way, at a rather later age, if no small brother or sister has appeared, the child's wish for a playmate, such as he has seen in other families, may gain the upper hand.

At the instigation of these feelings and worries, the child now comes to be occupied with the first, grand problem of life and asks himself the question: *'Where do babies come from?'* - a question which, there can be no doubt, first ran: 'Where did this particular, intruding baby come from?' We seem to hear the echoes of this first riddle in innumerable riddles of myth and legend. The question itself is, like all research, the product of a vital exigency, as though thinking were entrusted with the task of preventing the recurrence of such dreaded events. Let us assume, however, that the child's thinking soon becomes independent of this instigation, and henceforward goes on operating as a self-sustained instinct for research. Where a child is not already too much intimidated, he sooner or later adopts the direct method of demanding an answer from his parents or those in charge of him, who are in his eyes the source of all knowledge. This method, however, fails. The child receives either evasive answers or a rebuke for his curiosity, or he is dismissed with the mythologically significant piece of information which, in German countries, runs: 'The stork brings the babies; it fetches them out of the water.' I have reason to believe that far more children than their parents suspect are dissatisfied with this solution and meet it with energetic doubts, which, however, they do not always openly admit. I know of a three-year-old boy who, after receiving this piece of enlightenment, disappeared - to the terror of his nurse. He was found at the edge of the big pond adjoining the country house, to which he had hurried in order to see the babies in the water. I also know of another boy who could only allow his disbelief to find expression in a hesitant remark that he knew better, that it was not a stork that brought babies but a heron. It seems to me to follow from a great deal of information I have received that children refuse to believe the stork theory and that from the time of this first deception and rebuff they nourish a distrust of adults and have a suspicion of there being something forbidden which is being withheld from them by the 'grown-ups', and that they consequently hide their further researches under a cloak of secrecy. With this, however, the child also experiences the first occasion for a 'psychical conflict', in that views for which he feels an instinctual kind of preference, but which are not 'right' in the eyes of the grown-ups, come into opposition with other views, which are supported by the authority of the grown-ups without being acceptable to him himself. Such a psychical conflict may soon turn into a 'psychical dissociation'. The set of views which are bound up with being 'good', but also with a cessation of reflection, become the dominant and conscious views; while the other set, for which the child's work of research has meanwhile obtained fresh evidence, but which are not supposed to count, become the suppressed and 'unconscious' ones. The nuclear complex of a neurosis is in this way brought into being.

Recently, the analysis of a five-year-old boy, which his father undertook and which he has handed over to me for publication, has given me irrefutable proof of the correctness of a view towards which the psycho-analysis of adults had long been leading me. I now know that the change which takes place in the mother during pregnancy does not escape the child's sharp eyes and that he is very well able before long to establish the true connection between the increase in his mother's stoutness and the appearance of the baby. In the case just mentioned the boy was three and a half years old when his sister was born and four and three quarters when he showed his better knowledge by the most unmistakable allusions. This precocious discovery, however, is always kept secret, and later, in conformity with the further vicissitudes of the child's sexual researches, it is repressed and forgotten.

The 'stork fable', therefore, is not one of the sexual theories of children. On the contrary, it is the child's observation of animals, who hide so little of their sexual life and to whom he feels so closely akin, that strengthens his disbelief in it. With his knowledge, independently obtained, that babies grow inside the mother's body, he would be on the right road to solving the problem on which he first tries out his powers of thinking. But this further progress is inhibited by a piece of ignorance which cannot be made good and by false theories which the state of his own sexuality imposes on him.

These false sexual theories, which I shall now discuss, all have one very curious characteristic. Although they go astray in a grotesque fashion, yet each one of them contains a fragment of real truth; and in this they are analogous to the attempts of adults, which are looked at as strokes of genius, at solving the problems of the universe which are too hard for human comprehension. What is correct and hits the mark in such theories is to be explained by their origin from the components of the sexual instinct which are already stirring in the childish organism. For it is not owing to any arbitrary mental act or to chance impressions that those notions arise, but to the necessities of the child's psychosexual constitution; and this is why we can speak of sexual theories in children as being typical, and why we find the same mistaken beliefs in every child whose sexual life is accessible to us.

The first of these theories starts out from the neglect of the differences between the sexes on which I laid stress at the beginning of this paper as being characteristic of children. It consists in *attributing to everyone, including females, the possession of a penis*, such as the boy knows from his own body. It is precisely in what we must regard as the 'normal' sexual constitution that already in childhood the penis is the leading erotogenic zone and the chief auto-erotic sexual object; and the boy's estimate of its value is logically reflected in his inability to imagine a person like himself who is without this essential constituent. When a small boy sees his little sister's genitals, what he says shows that his prejudice is already strong enough to falsify his perception. He does not comment on the absence of a penis, but *invariably* says, as though by way of consolation and to put things right: 'Her ---'s still quite small. But when she gets bigger it'll grow all right.' The idea of a woman with a penis returns in later life, in the dreams of adults: the dreamer, in a state of nocturnal sexual excitation, will throw a woman down, strip her and prepare for intercourse - and then, in place of the female genitals, he beholds a well-developed penis and breaks off the dream and the excitation. The numerous hermaphrodites of classical antiquity faithfully reproduce this idea, universally held in childhood; one may observe that to most normal people they cause no offence, while the real hermaphroditic formations of the genitals which are permitted to occur by Nature nearly always excite the greatest abhorrence.

If this idea of a woman with a penis becomes 'fixated' in an individual when he is a child, resisting all the influences of later life and making him as a man unable to do without a penis in his sexual object, then, although in other respects he may lead a normal sexual life, he is bound to become a homosexual, and will seek his sexual object among men who, owing to some other physical and mental characteristics, remind him of women. Real women, when he comes to know them later, remain impossible as sexual objects for him, because they lack the essential sexual attraction; indeed, in connection with another impression of his childhood life, they may even become abhorrent to him. The child, having been mainly dominated by excitations in the penis, will usually have obtained pleasure by stimulating it with his hand; he will have been detected in this by his parents or nurse and terrorized by the threat of having his penis cut off. The effect of this 'threat of castration' is proportionate to the value set upon that organ and is quite extraordinarily deep and persistent. Legends and myths testify to the upheaval in the child's emotional life and to the horror which is linked with the castration complex - a complex which is subsequently remembered by consciousness with corresponding reluctance. The woman's genitalia, when seen later on, are regarded as a mutilated organ and recall this threat, and they therefore arouse horror instead of pleasure in the homosexual. This reaction cannot be altered in any way when the homosexual comes to learn from science that his childish assumption that women had a penis too was not so far wrong after all. Anatomy has recognized the clitoris within the female pudenda as being an organ that is homologous to the penis; and the physiology of the sexual processes has been able to add that this small penis which does not grow any bigger behaves in fact during childhood like a real and genuine penis - that it becomes the seat of excitations which lead to its being touched, that its excitability gives the little girl's sexual activity a masculine character and that a wave of repression in the years of puberty is needed in order for this masculine sexuality to be discarded and the woman to emerge. Since the sexual function of many women is crippled, whether by their obstinate clinging on to this excitability of the clitoris so that they remain anaesthetic in intercourse, or by such excessive repression occurring that its operation is partly replaced by hysterical compensatory formations - all this seems to show that there is some truth in the infantile sexual theory that women, like men, possess a penis.

It is easy to observe that little girls fully share their brother's opinion of it. They develop a great interest in that part of the boy's body. But this interest promptly falls under the sway of envy. They feel themselves unfairly treated. They make attempts to micturate in the posture that is made possible for boys by their possessing a big penis; and when a girl declares that 'she would rather be a boy', we know what deficiency her wish is intended to put right.

If children could follow the hints given by the excitation of the penis they would get a little nearer to the solution of their problem. That the baby grows inside the mother's body is obviously not a sufficient explanation. How does it get inside? What starts its development? That the father has something to do with it seems likely; he says that the baby is *his* baby as well.[1] Again, the penis certainly has a share, too, in these mysterious happenings; the excitation in it which accompanies all these activities of the child's thoughts bears witness to this. Attached to this excitation are impulsions which the child cannot account for - obscure urges to do something violent, to press in, to knock to pieces, to tear open a hole somewhere. But when the child thus seems to be well on the way to postulating the existence of the vagina and to concluding that an incursion of this kind by his father's penis into his mother is the act by means of which the baby is created in his mother's body - at this juncture his enquiry is broken off in helpless perplexity. For standing in its way is his theory that his mother possesses a penis just as a man does, and the existence of the cavity which receives the penis remains undiscovered by him. It is not hard to guess that the lack of success of his intellectual efforts makes it easier for him to reject and forget them. This brooding and doubting, however, becomes the prototype of all later intellectual work directed towards the solution of problems, and the first failure has a crippling effect on the child's whole future.

[1] Cf. the 'Analysis of a Five-Year-Old Boy' (1909*b*).

Their ignorance of the vagina also makes it possible for children to believe in the second of their sexual theories. If the baby grows in the mother's body and is then removed from it, this can only happen along the one possible pathway -the anal aperture. *The baby must be evacuated like a piece of excrement, like a stool.* When, in later childhood, the same question is the subject of solitary reflection or of a discussion between two children, the explanations probably arrived at are that the baby emerges from the navel, which comes open, or that the abdomen is slit up and the baby taken out - which was what happened to the wolf in the story of Little Red Riding-Hood. These theories are expressed aloud and also consciously remembered later on; they no longer contain anything objectionable. These same children have by then completely forgotten that in earlier years they believed in another theory of birth, which is now obstructed by the repression of the anal sexual components that has meanwhile occurred. At that time a motion was something which could be talked about in the nursery without shame. The child was still not so distant from his constitutional coprophilic inclinations. There was nothing degraded about coming into the world like a heap of faeces, which had not yet been condemned by feelings of disgust. The cloacal theory, which, after all, is valid for so many animals, was the most natural theory, and it alone could obtrude upon the child as being a probable one.

This being so, however, it was only logical that the child should refuse to grant women the painful prerogative of giving birth to children. If babies are born through the anus, then a man can give birth just as well as a woman. It is therefore possible for a boy to imagine that he, too, has children of his own, without there being any need to accuse him on that account of having feminine inclinations. He is merely giving evidence in this of the anal erotism which is still alive in him.

If the cloacal theory of birth is preserved in consciousness during later years of childhood, as occasionally happens, it is accompanied too by a solution - no longer, it is true, a primary one - of the problem of the origin of babies. Here it is like being in a fairy story; one eats some particular thing and gets a child from it. This infantile theory of birth is revived in cases of insanity. A manic woman, for instance, will lead the visiting doctor to a little heap of faeces which she has deposited in a corner of her cell, and say to him with a laugh: 'That's the baby I had to-day.'

The third of the typical sexual theories arises in children if, through some chance domestic occurrence, they become witnesses of sexual intercourse between their parents. Their perceptions of what is happening are bound, however, to be only very incomplete. Whatever detail it may be that comes under their observation - whether it is the relative positions of the two people, or the noises they make, or some accessory circumstance - children arrive in every case at the same conclusion. They adopt what may be called a *sadistic view of coition*. They see it as something that the stronger participant is forcibly inflicting on the weaker, and they (especially boys) compare it to the romping familiar to them from their childish experience - romping which, incidentally, is not without a dash of sexual excitation. I have not been able to ascertain that children recognize this behaviour which they have witnessed between their parents as the missing link needed for solving the problem of babies; it appears more often that the connection is overlooked by them for the very reason that they have interpreted the act of love as an act of violence. But this view of it itself gives an impression of being a return of the obscure impulse towards cruel behaviour which became attached to the excitations of the child's penis when he first began to think about the problem of where babies came from. The possibility, too, cannot be excluded that this premature sadistic impulse, which might so nearly have led to the discovery of coition, itself first emerged under the influence of extremely obscure memories of parental intercourse, for which the child had obtained the material - though at the time he made no use of it - while he was still in his first years and was sharing his parents' bedroom.[1]

[1] Restif de la Bretonne, in his autobiographical work *Monsiur Nocholas* (1794), tells a story of an impression he received at the

age of four, which confirms this sadistic misunderstanding of coitus.

The sadistic theory of coitus which, taken in isolation, is misleading where it might have provided confirmatory evidence, is, once again, the expression of one of the innate components of the sexual instinct, any of which may be strongly marked to a greater or lesser degree in each particular child. For this reason the theory is correct up to a certain point; it has in part divined the nature of the sexual act and the 'sex-battle' that precedes it. Not infrequently, too, the child is in a position to support this view by accidental observations which he understands in part correctly, but also in part incorrectly and indeed in a reversed sense. In many marriages the wife does in fact recoil from her husband's embraces, which bring her no pleasure, but the risk of a fresh pregnancy. And so the child who is believed to be asleep (or who is pretending to be asleep) may receive an impression from his mother which he can only interpret as meaning that she is defending herself against an act of violence. At other times the whole marriage offers an observant child the spectacle of an unceasing quarrel, expressed in loud words and unfriendly gestures; so that he need not be surprised if the quarrel is carried on at night as well, and finally settled by the same method which he himself is accustomed to use in his relations with his brothers and sisters or playmates.

Moreover, if the child discovers spots of blood in his mother's bed or on her underclothes, he regards it as a confirmation of his view. It proves to him that his father has made another similar assault on his mother during the night (whereas we should rather take the fresh spots of blood to mean that there had been a temporary cessation of sexual intercourse). Much of the otherwise inexplicable 'horror of blood' shown by neurotics finds its explanation from this connection. Once again, however, the child's mistake contains a fragment of truth. For in certain familiar circumstances a trace of blood is in fact judged as a sign that sexual intercourse has been begun.

A question connected somewhat indirectly with the insoluble problem of where babies come from also engages the child - the question as to the nature and content of the state called 'being married'; and he answers the question differently according as his chance perceptions in relation to his parents have coincided with instincts of his own which are still pleasurably coloured. All that these answers seem to have in common is that the child promises himself pleasurable satisfaction from being married and supposes that it involves a disregard of modesty. The notion I have most frequently met with is that *each of the married couple urinate in front of the other*. A variation of this, which sounds as if it was meant to indicate a greater knowledge symbolically, is that *the man urinates into the woman's chamber-pot*. In other instances the meaning of marriage is supposed to be that *the two people show their behinds to each other* (without being ashamed). In one case, in which education had succeeded in postponing sexual knowledge especially late, a fourteen-year-old girl, who had already begun to menstruate, arrived from the books she had read at the idea that being married consisted in a 'mixing of blood'; and since her own sister had not yet started her periods, the lustful girl made an assault on a female visitor who had confessed that she was just then menstruating, so as to force her to take part in this 'blood mixing'.

Childhood opinions about the nature of marriage, which are not seldom retained by conscious memory, have great significance for the symptomatology of later neurotic illness. At first they find expression in children's games in which each child does with another whatever it is that in his view constitutes being married; and then, later on, the wish to be married may choose the infantile form of expression and so make its appearance in a phobia which is at first sight unrecognizable, or in some corresponding symptom.[1]

These seem to be the most important of the typical sexual theories that children produce spontaneously in early childhood, under the sole influence of the components of the sexual instinct. I know that I have not succeeded in making my material complete or in establishing an unbroken connection between it and the rest of infantile life. But I may add one or two supplementary observations, whose absence would otherwise be noticed by any well-informed person. Thus, for instance, there is the significant theory that a baby is got by a kiss - a theory which obviously betrays the predominance of the erotogenic zone of the mouth. In my experience this theory is exclusively feminine and is sometimes found to be pathogenic in girls whose sexual researches have been subjected to exceedingly strong inhibitions in childhood. Again, through an accidental observation, one of my women patients happened upon the theory of the 'couvade', which, as is well known, is a general custom among some races and is probably intended to contradict the doubts as to paternity which can never be entirely overcome. A rather eccentric uncle of this patient's stayed at home for days after the birth of his child and received visitors in his dressing-gown, from which she concluded that both parents took part in the birth of their children and had to go to bed.

[1] The games that are most significant for subsequent neuroses are playing at 'doctor' and at 'father and mother'.

In about their tenth or eleventh year, children get to hear about sexual matters. A child who has grown up in a comparatively uninhibited social atmosphere, or who has found better opportunities for observation, tells other children what he knows, because this makes him feel mature and superior. What children learn in this way is mostly correct - that is, the existence of the vagina and its purpose is revealed to them; but otherwise the explanations they get from one another are not infrequently mixed with false ideas and burdened with remains of the older infantile sexual theories. They are scarcely ever complete or sufficient to solve the primordial problem. Just as formerly it was ignorance of the vagina which prevented the whole process from being understood, so now is it ignorance of the semen. The child cannot guess that another substance besides urine is excreted from the male sexual organ, and occasionally an 'innocent' girl on her wedding night is still indignant at her husband 'urinating into her'. This information acquired in the years of pre-puberty is followed by a new access of sexual researches by the child. But the theories which he now produces no longer have the typical and original stamp which was characteristic of the primary theories of early childhood as long as the infantile sexual components could find expression in theories in an uninhibited and unmodified fashion. The child's later intellectual efforts at solving the puzzles of sex have not seemed to me worth collecting, nor can they have much claim to a pathogenic significance. Their multiplicity is of course mainly dependent on the nature of the enlightenment which a child receives; but their significance consists rather in the fact that they re-awaken the traces, which have since become unconscious, of his first period of sexual interest; so that it is not infrequent for masturbatory sexual activity and some degree of emotional detachment from his parents to be linked up with them. Hence the condemnatory judgement of teachers that enlightenment of such a kind at this age 'corrupts' children.

Let me give a few examples to show what elements often enter into these late speculations by children about sexual life. A girl had heard from her schoolmates that the husband gives his wife an egg, which she hatches out in her body. A boy, who had also heard of the egg, identified it with the testicle, which [in German] is vulgarly called by the same word [*Ei*]; and he racked his brains to make out how the contents of the scrotum could be constantly renewed. The information given seldom goes far enough to prevent important uncertainties about sexual events. Thus a girl may arrive at an expectation that intercourse occurs on one occasion only, but that it lasts a very long time - twenty-four hours - and that all the successive babies come from this single occasion. One would suppose that this child had got her knowledge of the reproductive process from certain insects; but it turned out that this was not so and that the theory emerged as a spontaneous creation. Other girls are ignorant of the period of gestation, the life in the womb, and assume that the baby appears immediately after the first night of intercourse. Marcel Prevost has turned this girlhood mistake into an amusing story in one of his '*Lettres de femmes*'. These later sexual researches of children, or of adolescents who have been retarded at the stage of childhood, offer an almost inexhaustible theme and one which is perhaps not uninteresting in general; but it is more remote from my present interest. I must only lay stress on the fact that in this field children produce many incorrect ideas in order to contradict older and better knowledge which has become unconscious and is repressed.

The way in which children react to the information they are given also has its significance. In some, sexual repression has gone so far that they will not listen to anything; and these succeed in remaining ignorant even in later life - *apparently* ignorant, at least - until, in the psycho-analysis of neurotics, the knowledge that originated in early childhood comes to light. I also know of two boys between ten and thirteen years old who, though it is true that they listened to the sexual information, rejected it with the words: ' *Your* father and other people may do something like that, but I know for certain *my* father never would.' But however widely children's later reactions to the satisfaction of their sexual curiosity may vary, we may assume that in the first years of childhood their attitude was absolutely uniform, and we may feel certain that at that time all of them tried most eagerly to discover what it was that their parents did with each other so as to produce babies.